What

Compiled by L.D. Lewis

ALL RIGHTS RESERVED 2015

Foreword

What a gift when one person passes down something of significant value! Sharing not only the object, but the story behind it as well. That's how I feel about the Christmas legacy that has been gifted and passed down to me. Not just by celebrating the "season" but being honored enough to know the TRUE meaning of Christmas, and to have the privilege of passing it down to my own children and grandchildren, should the Lord tarry.

Being raised in a Christian home, Christmas was a major part of my life. No Santa, no North Pole, no elves... We don't even know for sure if December 25th is the right day of His birth, but it doesn't matter. All I know is; He WAS born, and that gives reason for great celebration. So transforming and revolutionary was his entrance into my heart that I yearn to know more about my Saviour. We should celebrate Christmas all year Long!

I remember one time, as a little girl, I came home from school with a paper that said x-mas and my dear Mom said "Don't ever write that! We never take Christ out of Christmas" and it has stuck with me to this day. Every time I see that, my heart wrenches, and I feel like that's where we are in this time that we live in. So many have taken Christ out of Christmas and commercialized it to the point that they never stop and take the time to focus on what really matters.

Let's reflect on the first Christmas for a bit. Just imagine as the angel Gabriel was summoned to the very throne of the Almighty God to be sent to the little town of Nazareth to declare the greatest salutation to ever reach the earth to a simple Galilean girl. I can just see Gabriel plunging earthward, breaking every barrier from the supernatural to the natural world. I can see him sailing past all the stars that God calls each and every one by name. Slowing down, he reaches the little town of Nazareth to make a visit to a young virgin named Mary, espoused to a man named Joseph. "Hail, you who are highly favored, the Lord is with you: blessed art thou among women...Thou shalt bring forth a son, and thou shalt call his name JESUS." How stunned, yet humbled, Mary must have felt to be told that she would carry the very Son of the Most High God, not only His son, but her own Saviour, Jesus, Oh what a name! In His name, mountains shall be moved, people will be healed, lives saved and delivered from the most wretched of sins. The one name, that at the end of time, every knee shall bow and every tongue confess that Jesus Christ is Lord! What a glorious day that will be when the true meaning of Christmas, the Greatest Gift to this world, will be ours to behold for eternity. What a hope we have in Him! As we sit around the fireplace drinking our hot chocolate; while the snow is falling outside, let's take time to reflect on what Christ done for us by being willing to come to this earth as a babe in a lowly manger to take on the sins of this old world. Let the snow remind us of how His precious blood can fall on the blackest of sins and they become as white as the snow.

We want to thank each and every one for purchasing this book that our church people have so lovingly put together of what Christmas means to them. We want to thank Bro. Lewis for having the burden to put this together and for supporting the widows in our church from the proceeds of this book.

As you pass down family traditions, our prayer is that this book will become one of them. Sharing many stories of love, laughter, miracles and hope. To introduce someone to Jesus Christ and His word would be the greatest gift you could ever give someone this holiday season. Let's make a difference!

God Bless,

Sis. Stephanie Conner

Editor's Note

I appreciate all of the time and effort that the members from Hilldale Holiness Church spent writing material for this book.

I tried to keep editing to the minimum to preserve the feel of each writer. Every effort was made to preserve the original thought or idea when editing was necessary.

If there are mistakes or errors, I freely take credit (or blame) for them.

I hope you enjoy reading this book and, if you like clean Christian-based fiction books; I have six of them available on Amazon.com:

The Offer
The Deal
The Contract
The Vow

Two Edged Sword
Bittersweet

Feel free to contact me at:
lowelldlewis@gmail.com

Best Regards,
L.D. Lewis

What Christmas Means to Me

The Real Christmas Story

Luke 2:1-21

And it came to pass in those days, that there went out a decree from Caesar Augustus, that all the world should be taxed.

(And this taxing was first made when Cyrenius was governor of Syria.)

And all went to be taxed, every one into his own city.

And Joseph also went up from Galilee, out of the city of Nazareth, into Judaea, unto the city of David, which is called Bethlehem; (because he was of the house and lineage of David:)

To be taxed with Mary his espoused wife, being great with child.

And so it was, that, while they were there, the days were accomplished that she should be delivered.

And she brought forth her firstborn son, and wrapped him in swaddling clothes, and laid him in a manger; because there was no room for them in the inn.

And there were in the same country shepherds abiding in the field, keeping watch over their flock by night.

And, lo, the angel of the Lord came upon them, and the glory of the Lord shone round about them: and they were sore afraid.

And the angel said unto them, Fear not: for, behold, I bring you good tidings of great joy, which shall be to all people.

For unto you is born this day in the city of David a Saviour, which is Christ the Lord.

And this *shall be* a sign unto you; Ye shall find the babe wrapped in swaddling clothes, lying in a manger.

And suddenly there was with the angel a multitude of the heavenly host praising God, and saying,

Glory to God in the highest, and on earth peace, good will toward men.

And it came to pass, as the angels were gone away from them into heaven, the shepherds said one to another, Let us now go even unto Bethlehem, and see this thing which is come to pass, which the Lord hath made known unto us.

And they came with haste, and found Mary, and Joseph, and the babe lying in a manger.

And when they had seen *it,* they made known abroad the saying which was told them concerning this child.

And all they that heard *it* wondered at those things which were told them by the shepherds.

But Mary kept all these things, and pondered *them* in her heart.

And the shepherds returned, glorifying and praising God for all the things that they had heard and seen, as it was told unto them.

And when eight days were accomplished for the circumcising of the child, his name was called JESUS, which was so named of the angel before he was conceived in the womb.

What Christmas Means to Me

Before we got saved it was just another day where you open gifts and eat too much. Yes, we believed there was a man called Jesus, but we didn't know Him.

After we came to know Him as our Saviour, it was no longer just another day; but it was our Lord and Saviour's birthday.

By Douglas and Linda Farmer

Did you know?
The Germans made the first artificial Christmas trees out of dyed goose feathers.

Remember the Reason

As Christians, Christmas should be a joyful time; a time of celebration—a time of remembering the miracle of the Christmas Babe in the manger.

Why then does it feel so stressful? The shopping, cooking, planning, decorating, baking, and 101 things to be done. I enjoy all of those things and I look forward to Christmas—but sometimes I wonder; is Jesus pleased with all this?

Why do we do these things? Is it for Jesus? It is His birthday after all.

It is so easy to get caught up in the Christmas Season and forget the real reason we celebrate it.

Take time out from your busy schedule this year to remember Jesus. Take time to thank Him for coming as a baby. Give Him some extra time and attention in worship and praise. Take time to commune with Him and draw nearer in prayer. Just as we do with a loved one who has a birthday. We give them extra attention and do special things for them. We make sure they know we love them and we celebrate them!

Celebrate Jesus this Christmas! Let Him know how special He is and how glad you are He was born!
Remember the Reason!

By Charity Lewis

What Christmas Means to Me

This is what Christmas means to me: Celebrating the birth of Jesus by spending time with family and friends. Also, giving gifts in remembrance of Jesus being willing to be the greatest gift for us. I always look forward to the Christmas dinner as well. My very favorite food is mashed potatoes and brown gravy!

We always spend Christmas Eve at my Great Aunt Nannie's house enjoying time with our family.

I want to thank my mom and dad, my Nana and Papa Suit, the rest of my family, and Hilldale Holiness Church for always making Christmas so special for me.

That's what Christmas means to me.

By Zach Conner (Age 11)

What does Christmas mean to you? Take a moment and write it down in the space provided below.

Christmas Memories and Traditions

A Special Christmas

One of our most memorable Christmases was the one in which we were having the hardest year financially. Our two daughters were about 10 and 4 years old. So we decided to have a homemade Christmas.

Steve began making many trips with the girls to a ceramic shop and they picked out a set of canisters for me. I was decorating my kitchen in "cows" at the time, so that's the kind they got. Steve also picked out a "cow" clock and spoon holder for the stove. They had so much fun going with dad, and some of the time they brought the items home and did the painting in secret where I couldn't see what they were doing. They stored the ceramics in Jennifer's closet and she would stop me from going in her bedroom to put her clothes away.

I started my own projects; sewing things for them. I had a cutting board that I would stand up in the living room like a room divider and work behind it. The curiosity was high; which made it all the more fun. I made Anna a doll. She had always wanted one that you could put a real pacifier in its mouth. It was a challenge, but I did it and she named him Andy. Her Papa Case's name was Asa Andrew, and if we would have had a son, we were going to name him Stephen Andrew and call him Andy.

Christmas morning was beyond any we had ever had before. We were all excited to give our homemade gifts to each other. And, of course, the girls were so proud that they had helped make the canisters just for me. They were adorable! Steve added a personal touch to the "cow" clock he painted by putting our initials on it: SC+SC. That made it extra special. It just goes to show you don't have to spend a lot of money to make special memories and have a happy time together.

By Steve and Sharon Case

I remember one time that my mom got brick-looking paper and built a wood frame fireplace to put it on. (I think it was around Christmas time).

By Catherine M. Tosh

One year at Christmas time—I had only been saved a month or two—some young people and I went to church one night. I guess it might have had something to do with Christmas (anyway, no adults were there). It meant a lot to me, I guess, to be included (because I still remember it, and it is special to me). I think of it sometimes now when young people are practicing or getting together for their Christmas plays and activities.

By Catherine M. Tosh

When our boys, David and James, were young, I would wrap their presents and put them under the tree (we always had a Christmas tree).

They told us (after they were older) that when we were gone, they would carefully unwrap their presents and play with them—and then wrap them back up before we came back home.

We didn't know this until after they were grown and married.

One year when they were a little older, we bought .22 rifles for them for Christmas. We left the house for a while; when we returned, they were smiling like the cat that ate the canary. We had left the rifles out, unwrapped, on our bed. And, of course, they (being nosey as usual) found them!

There again, they told us all of this *after they were married.*

By Douglas and Linda Farmer

I was told that one Christmas my mom, dad, aunt, and (maybe) my uncle, carved presents out of bars of soap.

I'm guessing that times were hard.

By Catherine M. Tosh

One Christmas after mom and dad had remarried each other—and I had gotten saved (at age 15), Christmas Day fell on a Wednesday. We had presents to open, but my parents waited until I got back from church to open them. I appreciated that.

By Catherine M. Tosh

Christmas! What an exciting and special time it was as a child! Mama loved Christmas and always made it special. Looking back, I know there were hard times when we didn't have much, but as a child I never realized and don't remember those times. I remember family being together, good food, making candy, laughter, keeping secrets, Christmas plays, parades, music and lights.

Christmas Sunday was always special and something I looked forward to.

It was our family tradition to always open our gifts on Christmas Eve. We would all gather in the living room around the tree. Daddy would sit in his recliner with all four of us girls around him. He would pick up his Bible and read us the Christmas Story from Luke Chapter 2. Many times I heard my daddy's voice break and saw him moved to tears by the wonderful and miraculous story of Jesus coming to earth as a lowly babe in a manger.

Then daddy would pray and mom would start passing out gifts. It was a wonderful happy time.

The years have passed and all of us girls have gone our separate ways, with children of our own. Daddy is home with Jesus now.

I'll never forget the first Christmas after daddy passed away; he wasn't there to read us the Christmas Story. Someone else had to read it and we all cried—remembering and missing daddy. Hearing him read the Story of Christmas is a precious memory I will always treasure.

We don't always get to be together at Christmas now; but when we do, we read the story of Christmas from the Bible and remember why we have Christmas in the first place—and then turn our hearts and minds to the wonderful gift He was and still is to us today.

By Charity Lewis

I remember that when my dad was alive, Loren and I would take turns going either to my parent's house for

Christmas, or to Loren's mom and stepdad's home. We had no problem with that arrangement. (Loren's dad died before we got married).

After my dad died, mom became bedfast (or homebound), because of emphysema. At Christmas, we'd go see her and I'd fix food. We would visit for a while and then we would go to Loren's mom and stepdad's home.

Loren had nine siblings. I remember on Christmas, when we went to his mom's house, there were so many people that some would have to sleep on the floor on blankets and others on air mattresses that oftentimes went flat (which made us laugh!).

They only had two bedrooms and two beds in their home.

During this time, I loved to smell the turkey cooking in the oven during the night.

After Loren died, I lived with my daughter, Cathy, and her husband, Brent. Sometimes at Christmas my children and their families would gather at Brent and Cathy's home. After eating Christmas dinner, we would open our Christmas gifts.

Their house is very small and some folks would end up sitting on the living room floor to open presents.

After the presents had been opened and wrapping paper was strewn all around, they would make balls out of the paper and have a Christmas wrapping-paper ball war. It seemed like everyone really enjoyed that more than the gifts!

I wasn't worried about anything getting broken because it was just paper being thrown around.

By Catherine M. Tosh

Since a child, Christmas has always been a special day for me! I am glad the church I was raised in did talk about the birth of Jesus—the one who came to save our lost souls.

Being one of five children, we were of meager means. Dad and mom were loved and respected by us children— and I never felt bad about being poor.

We were taught that there was right and wrong; and that we were supposed to work, and work hard. We did not expect to be taken care of by our government. Honest work was a moral issue.

Christmas was exciting! Mom was a real good cook. Sometimes we would receive one gift because times were hard.

The first time I gave my heart to Jesus, I was eight years old; that was 64 years ago. I left the Lord for many years, but in 1970, I got saved in a Free Will Baptist Church. In August 1972, my wife, our two daughters and I received the Baptism of the Holy Ghost in an Assembly of God Church in Sand Springs, Oklahoma, where Rev. Lawrence Lewis was the pastor.

Life really changed for us; I really began to know who Jesus is, was, and forever will be.

Christmas has changed, but it is still special. I am saddened to see the change over the years—how children don't really know who Jesus is.

In our country, Jesus has been taken out of Christmas, prayer, schools, government, and even some of our churches. I am not politically correct. I am not ashamed of Jesus Christ. He will come back again and take those who have been saved by His blood back to Heaven with Him—that will be a real Christmas!

By Bro. Spencer Conner

Mama, Its Santa Claus

Thinking back, I have a lot of memories—especially of Christmases past.

My mother died when I was nine, leaving my daddy with four of us kids, the oldest eleven, so we didn't have a bunch of toys at Christmas.

We had wood stoves, but no fireplace to hang our stockings on. We had good times when my uncle, aunt and their family all came to see us and stay all night with us on Christmas Eve. All of us kids slept on pallets in the front room—we talked, laughed and giggled. We could hardly wait for the next morning.

When I was little, all of us girls wore long, light brown, cotton stockings. On Christmas Eve, we would all hang them up on the wall behind the big warm wood stove. The boys found their daddy's longest socks to hang. We could hardly sleep. We were all together on our warm pallets; anxious to see what was in our stockings the next morning.

After we were all asleep, our mamas filled the stockings with candy, nuts, oranges and apples. We had such a good Christmas morning to wake up to. And then, we'd have a big dinner with lots of family.

Since I've grown up now, with a big family of my own; they all come to my house for Christmas Eve. There's lots of laughing and talking. We are glad to be together.

One of my favorite memories is when W.D. (my late husband) and I invited my sister and her husband, Ed, over one cold Christmas Eve night. Ed was heavy built and made a good Santa Claus. He had a real nice Santa suit. He didn't come in with my sister, but waited until we were all sitting around in the front room. All of the kids were on the floor, waiting to open presents, when the dogs started barking. My kids were grown and didn't know Santa was coming. My baby boy, Marty Dale, opened the front door and, coming through the gate was Santa, hollering "Ho, ho, ho!" Marty turned around and looked at me with such a surprised, serious, and puzzled, look and said, "Mama, its Santa Claus." It was precious to me.

The Lord has blessed me with a lot of good memories.

By LaVera Clements

My Best Christmas Ever

It was 2003. I had just turned six years old. It was Christmas Eve. My dad had tucked me into bed. I asked him if he would help me pray—because I wanted to ask Jesus into my heart. Dad and mom prayed together with me, and that is when I became a Christian.

By Zachary Stickler

Making Christmas Special

Looking back on my childhood Christmases, I find that the things that I remember are not the "*presents*" I received; but the "*presence*" of my family and the things we did together. I can't think of a Christmas as a child without thinking about my mama; because she is what made Christmas special at our house.

As I came into motherhood as a young lady, I realized that now I'm the mom and it's up to me to make Christmas special for my kids. Just putting up the Christmas tree, lights and decorations was exciting. My kids had a small tree in the kitchen that we let them decorate with mostly homemade decorations. Some years we would make snowflakes, string popcorn and gingerbread men.

After all the decorations were up and the house was transformed into a "magical place", I would spread a blanket on the floor in front of the tree where we would eat popcorn and drink hot chocolate "picnic style"—using only the light from the tree. Sometimes I would read a book aloud to the kids, or we would play a game. I often read short stories Lowell had written just for the kids.

I always made a lot of cookies at Christmas. Our family favorite is sugar cookies. I always let the kids have a few cookies to decorate. They had so much fun piling on the icing and sprinkles. As they got older, my girls would want to help make the cookies—and then it got to where they took over the whole project! I'm glad that they still enjoy doing it every year. Last year I made several batches of sugar cookies, and all of my grown up kids came over for an evening of decorating Christmas cookies. We had a wonderful time making memories.

The kids always liked for me to read to them out loud. During the Christmas season, sometimes in the evenings we'd turn out all the lights except the lights on the tree and I would read to them (Lowell could usually be found "snoozing" in his recliner nearby—but I think he really liked listening to the stories). When the kids were little, I only read small books by the tree, but when they got bigger, we would read chapter books—or even series'. One year I read the entire "Little House on the Prairie" series to them. Of course, they never wanted to stop. It was always "just one more chapter, mom!"

Now that my kids are grown up, Christmas is a little different, but I still like to try to make it special. We still decorate cookies together; work puzzles together, make candy together, and eat together. I have found that whatever we are doing; just being together is what makes it special.

By Charity Lewis

God's Mysterious Ways

One year Christmas was drawing near and again we were hitting it really close in our finances. I always liked to make Christmas as special as I could for my wife and girls; but this year, I had tried to get overtime; tried to find a second job—or even odd jobs, but nothing seemed to work out.

So, I found myself praying and saying, "God, if you don't help me, it looks like my girls are not going to get anything for Christmas this year."

One Saturday after that, I had gone rabbit hunting with a friend and we were having a hard time finding property we were looking for. We saw a man going to his mailbox with a beagle following along behind him, so we stopped to ask directions.

"That's a nice looking beagle you've got there," I said.

"He strayed in here a couple of weeks ago and nobody has come looking for him. I don't want him, so if you want him, take him," he said.

"Sure," I replied. "I'd love to!"

She was the best rabbit dog I've ever had. She would even fetch your rabbits back to you.

About a week before Christmas, I was hunting with a man and the dogs ran a rabbit by us. He shot at it and hit it, but it kept running.

Pretty soon the dogs stopped barking and the man said, "They must have lost it."

I replied, "No, my little female dog is probably bringing it back to you."

Sure enough, about that time, the little beagle came backing out of the brush, dragging the rabbit behind her. That man wanted my beagle so bad that he offered me enough money to buy all of my girls Christmas presents. God does work in mysterious ways!

By Steve Case

Christmas Traditions

We have held these traditions for as long as I can remember:

Every Christmas Eve we would go to my Pa and Nana Stickler's house. Pa and Nana would make candies and pies. Some of the pumpkin pies were made without pie crust because my Uncle Phil didn't like the crust.

We would eat all kinds of good food, and then my Pa would go get the Bible and read about the birth of Jesus Christ. After that we would open our gifts.

When we came home, my parents would let me open one stocking stuffer. I would be so excited on Christmas morning that I would wake up my parents so we could open presents. After we opened our family presents, we would go to my Papa and Grandma Young's house.

After Papa passed away, we started going to my Uncle Richard and Aunt Dana Huerta's house. We usually have turkey and dressing (my Aunt Dana makes the best dressing, by the way). Uncle Richard reads the Bible story about the birth of Jesus; and then we open our gifts.

A lot has changed in my eighteen years of life—with my Papa Young and Nana Stickler both passing away.

By Zachary Stickler

Our Last Christmas Together

The Christmas I remember the most was the Christmas of 2000. I didn't realize what the New Year would bring.

In January of 2000, Johnny, my late husband, was diagnosed with myelodysplasia (or smoldering leukemia).

In 2000, he spent a lot of time in the hospital having chemotherapy treatments and blood transfusions. We did that for almost the entire year.

So, the Christmas of 2000, when the weathermen started saying that we would have a white Christmas—our kids and grandkids came over because we were snowed in. What we didn't realize is that this would be the last Christmas we would all be together (Dana, Richard, Kylie, Drew, Ryan, Debbie, Marty, and Zach—were all there with us).

Johnny was so proud of his daughters and our sons-in-law—and his grandkids, who could do no wrong. He loved them so.

When 2001 came, everything went pretty good for him. He felt good and was able to spend a lot of time fishing with his brothers. We spent time fishing at Grove with our kids, just being together as a family. More times than not, Johnny would catch his limit of crappie, so we had lots of fish-fry's.

He would astonish the doctors. His blood count would be really low and they would ask how he was doing. He would tell them everything he had done: fishing; walking a long distance to get to where the crappie were biting; using a rotor tiller in a garden for his daughter, and putting out tomato plants. The doctors were amazed, and said that he should be laid out with no more blood than he had.

He would tell them that people were praying for him. He knew where his help came from; it came from Jesus.

On June 16th, 2001, he went to be with the One who had been his help here on earth.

God has been so good to us. I know one day we will all be together again.

By Sis. Sue Young

Taking Time to Care

Our girls love to bake and at Christmas time they enjoyed helping me bake cookies and candy. We would make up plates of our goodies and take them around to some of our neighbors. One of our neighbors was particularly poor and not very well liked on our street, but he was always happy to get the Christmas goodies. One year, he said, "I wondered if you girls were going to bring me some cookies and candy this year."

Anna also enjoyed baking goodies and taking a plate to the fire department to share with the local firemen.

One year, Anna wanted to make some cookies and take them to the homeless people. So she baked them up and put them on plates. Steve took her down to an area in downtown Tulsa where a lot of homeless people hang out. They passed them out to all the people they could find, but still had several left over. Anna asked her dad to drive her around to where the prostitutes were known to frequent. One particular "lady" was sitting on a rock wall waving to all the men that drove by, trying to get them to stop. Steve stopped and let Anna get out and go talk to the woman. I don't know what Anna said exactly, but after a few minutes, the woman was wiping tears and hugged Anna, thanking her for caring about her.

By Steve and Sharon Case

My Christmas Memory

I remember growing up in a small town in northwest Arkansas. My folks weren't rich by any means but my Dad worked hard and was a good provider for his family, the Lord had certainly blessed us. We always had plenty to eat, a nice home to live in and more clothes than we needed. My older brother and I always received several nice things for Christmas every year. I remember one year Mom had heard about a way to encourage your family to do good deeds for each other during the Christmas season. This is what we did: Mom got a small basket to use as a manger for baby Jesus; she cut yellow yarn into several small pieces to use as straw for the manger. Starting in December we would get to put one piece of yarn in the manger each time we did a good deed for someone in our family, the object was to make sure that baby Jesus had plenty of yarn in the manger before he was born on Christmas day. It was really fun trying to make sure that you did enough good deeds to fill the basket with yarn.

Another good memory that I have of Christmas, my Mom's brother and her two sisters and their kids and our family would all meet at my grandparent's house on Christmas Eve. We would enjoy a great meal, a lot of great fellowship then we would go into the living room, and sit around the fire. The first thing we would do is read the Christmas story in St. Luke then afterward we would open our presents, now that I have a family of my own we still read the Christmas story before we open our gifts, I don't ever want to forget the real reason for the Christmas season, JESUS CHRIST.

By Bro. Marty Stickler

It Makes Me Homesick

Going to *Granda Cordie's* house for Christmas was exciting to me when I was just a boy. She got the name Granda Cordie when my oldest sister, Karen, couldn't say "Grandma Cordia". I never knew her "real" name until I was almost a teenager.

We lived about two and a half hours away, but it seemed like a grand adventure to me—going to Granda Cordie's house. We lived in Shawnee, Oklahoma and she lived in Howe, Oklahoma. Howe was a small town in Eastern Oklahoma where downtown consisted of one block of small businesses, including a little grocery store—kind of like a Five and Dime. There was an Assembly of God Church (where Granda Cordie attended), a couple of other small churches, and a large old rock schoolhouse with a rock fence around the perimeter of the property. The top of the fence was wide enough that you could walk on it, if you were careful. You could see the schoolhouse and the rock fence from Granda Cordie's front porch.

Granda Cordie's house was an old white frame house that faced west, with a porch that ran across the front and a lean-to style carport on the left side of the house. There were several huge old oak trees that were scattered around the house, providing shade in the summer and dumping leaves on the ground in the fall. There was a two lane paved road, a railroad track, and another two lane road between her house and the school.

Granda Cordie always decorated her front windows with Christmas lights; and she put white plastic candles with orange bulbs in her front windows.

Going to Howe was always an adventure for me, because my dad would tell me stories of his childhood and of things that had happened.

When we would drive through Poteau, Oklahoma, on our way to Howe, he would point at Cavanal Hill and say, "That's the highest hill in the world. It is one foot short of being a mountain."

I would gaze out my window and wonder why they didn't haul a truckload of dirt up there and just make it a mountain.

"That's where I used to go fishing," he'd say, pointing to an overgrown creek.

I would look longingly at the creek; wishing we could fish there together.

"I had my picture taken on top of that bridge," he'd say.

I would stare in amazement and fear, thinking of climbing up on top of the steel beams of the bridge.

And then we would arrive at Granda Cordie's where we would be greeted with hugs and oohs and ah's at how tall we were getting and how much we were growing up (us kids, anyway). The house always smelled of ham and turkey, pecan and pumpkin pies, and other mouthwatering aromas from the kitchen.

In the formal dining room, on one wall there was an old clock that came from a train station from the railway where my Granddad Walter Lewis worked, and below it was an antique bureau (that I have in my living room today). On the wall to the right of the entry into the kitchen, there was a Cuckoo Clock; and every hour on the hour, a bird would slide out from a hole in the clock and make a lot of racket. I was half–scared of that clock when I was little. I wasn't sure if the bird was real or fake.

Christmas Eve, when all the family was gathered there at the house—after eating and opening presents, we kids would sleep on pallets on the floor in the living room. Granda Cordie would leave the Christmas lights on around her front windows, and the plastic candles in the windows would glow bright orange.

My memories of Christmas at Granda Cordie's are priceless. The food and laughter; the teasing, and the hugs; the stories of days gone by; hearing my Great Aunt Ilda exclaim "Oooooh!" as only she could; watching my cousin, Keith, play the piano Floyd Cramer or Jerry Lee Lewis style; hearing dad's voice catch when he prayed before we ate; seeing Granda Cordie's fake silver Christmas tree in the corner of the living room surrounded by presents; Aunt Neoma's peanut brittle (she knew how much I loved it and would often make me a special batch that was all mine); seeing Granda Cordie cooking at the stove; the hard Christmas candy that was always in a candy dish on the coffee table; the nights of lying in bed looking at the glow of Christmas lights from the porch and windows, wondering what presents awaited in our stockings in the morning.

Granddad Walter, Granda Cordie, Dad, Karen, Aunt Neoma and Aunt Ilda are all gone now—and the old home place has been sold to someone else—but the memories are as real and poignant as if they had all happened yesterday. I can still hear their voices and their laughter; I can smell the food and feel the ambience of the house. I sit here with tears in my eyes—remembering…and it makes me homesick. Oh, what a glorious homecoming awaits!

By L.D. Lewis

Spiritual Traditions

About 5 or 6 years ago, we started a "spiritual" tradition at Christmas time when all of our children and grandchildren are gathered around.

Steve always reads the Christmas story out loud—well, sometimes he can't finish reading the story for crying and someone else will finish it for him. It's a very special time for all of us. One year we decided to add another spiritual note to our Christmas celebration: I bought umbrellas for our two girls and tied their names, and the names of their family member, so that they hung from under the umbrellas. We told them this represented an "Umbrella of Prayer" that they were under each day. I saw Anna's at her house just a month ago. It made me smile.

The next year, we made "prayer cloths" out of red velvet material; shaped like hearts. Steve and I prayed over them and wrote each person's name on their prayer cloth and passed them out before we opened gifts.

One year we bought a small canvas picture that had the hands of God on it and the scripture in Isaiah 49:16 ..."Behold, I have inscribed you on the palms of my hands." Using transparent labels, I typed their names on them and put them in God's hands. I also still see those in the girls' homes. That year Ben Johnson and his boys spent Christmas with us, and every year our girls ask, "Are Ben and the boys going to be with us this year?" We always enjoy having them!

Another year, Steve wanted me to make a big red heart like a pillow. He talked to everyone there that year about loving God and His love for us by sending His Son. Then we passed the pillow around to everyone in the room with a felt marker and told them to write their name on the pillow if they love God and wanted to give Him their heart. It was unanimous!

Last year, we wrapped the most expensive gift of each one there in plain brown paper wrapping paper. We told them about how when Jesus came, even though He was the best gift ever, He came wrapped in plain wrapping. Not showy or fancy. Born in a humble setting, wrapped in swaddling clothes—He was the greatest gift of all!

Christmas is right around the corner, so we'll both be thinking and praying; "Lord, what can we do this year to help instill You and Your Word into our family?"

By Steve and Sharon Case

Together for Christmas

One Christmas that is special to our family is from 2007. That Christmas was different than the others. We were expecting a severe ice storm and my husband, Wade, was trying to make it home for Christmas (he drives a truck for a living).

We celebrated with my family on Christmas Eve night and the storm had begun. The kids and I headed home where we frantically waited for Wade to arrive. We had never spent a Christmas apart.

I was checking routes on the computer and talking with my husband—each highway that he came to would be open at the time I checked, and then closed when he arrived. He finally got re-routed to Highway 51 and Highway 75 and made it to the Town West area in Tulsa. My brother-in-law was able to drive over to pick up my husband; and we happily got to celebrate Christmas together as a family.

By Kindall, Chandler, and Lexy
Feeback

The Perfect Picture of Christmas

Presents! Presents everywhere! Nothing was more exciting to me as a little girl than walking into my great aunt's gift-filled living room on Christmas Eve. We children would carefully step over the colorfully wrapped boxes so we could hug our family. Smiles and laughter would quickly fill the energetic house, and children would be giggling as they'd try to guess which present was theirs. My aunts would prepare the food while my crazy uncles entertained the whole house. I remember looking intently at the dessert table and contemplating on sneaking a cookie before it was time to open presents. I stopped myself from taking the sugary treat in fear that I would get caught and that my present would be given to someone else.

At last, it was time to open gifts! There were so many presents to open. One by one, the gifts were handed out as I waited patiently on the floor for the box that had my name written across it. By the time the night was over, each of us grandkids had received a generous amount of gifts and we were all more than thrilled to receive such presents filled with love.

It was always a sad occasion when it was time to go home, but we all knew we would be back the next day to eat Christmas dinner together. As we gathered once again the next day, we came with an empty stomach so we could enjoy the enormous amounts of food to be had. When all had their fill, we played games and laughed as we talked in the living room. So much love always filled my Aunt Annie's house at Christmas time, and so much joy overflowed out of everyone's hearts.

When it was almost time to go, my mom would always sit down at the piano and call for my sister and I to come and sing a few songs for the family. Standing to the side of my mom while she played, my sister and I would sing the songs that so wonderfully conveyed the true meaning of Christmas. We never sang "Jingle Bells", or "Deck the Halls"; but instead, we sang, "O Holy Night", or Silent Night", and other songs that had the message of Christ's birth.

Watching my aunts tear up as I sang with my mom and sister, my mind would always drift to the Saviour who came down to Earth to give the greatest gift ever known; Himself. He's the reason we sing our songs and give gifts every year to our families and everyone else around us. But most of all, He's the reason for our salvation. He came down to this earth in the form of a baby boy to be placed in a manger. He died a horrible death for us and our sins thirty three years later. What an unconditional act of love! Jesus Christ may have died two thousand years ago, but He is not dead! He gloriously arose from the dead three days after His crucifixion and is still alive today. He may not be with us physically anymore, but I know He is alive within many hearts and lives, including my own.

Every year the world gathers together on Christmas Day—many not even knowing the true meaning of Christmas. However, we who do know can spread His love and the Gospel message so that He can be celebrated.

None of the gifts and food; nor the story of Santa Claus, can ever convey what Christmas means to me. The fact that God came down in the form of a man to save a sinful world, including myself, is the perfect picture of what Christmas means to me.

By Ashleigh Conner

Christmas Memories

As I sit here and try to think of my favorite Christmas memory to try to write about, I find that there are far too many to choose just one. Searching back over the years in my mind, I remember so much. One of my favorites is the gift we all got my mom in 1997. She decided she wanted a new front door. I know that sounds a bit odd, but my mother has always been very precise and particular when she gets it into her head that she wants something. So, she decided she wanted a door—a wood door, solid, not hollow, with a full oval window in it. I don't know about now, but I remember then that it was nearly impossible to locate such a door, so she pretty well gave up on the idea. My sister took on the task of locating a door for her, and finally found one—special made, at a lumber mill in Arkansas—for a lot of money.

We knew mom would never pay that for a door for herself, so all of us kids went together and bought her the door for Christmas—and that door is still on her house today. Everyone was there that Christmas Eve night, as we are every year, except for me. I was a dispatcher for the City of Tulsa at the time, and I had to work; however, they called me, and as I listened over the phone, I could hear everything as my brothers brought the door in for her. Needless to say, she was very happy—and very surprised! That was a very good Christmas. Also, it was around that time that we started having visits from Santa Claus every year. I'm talking red suit and all. This is something my mom, my Aunt Billie Fay, and my uncle Ed schemed up together without telling anyone else in the family. My brother, Marty, was standing closest to the front door. When he heard the gate open, and someone coming up the walk, he looked out the window, and then said, "Santa Claus is here!" Then he looked at momma, and said again, "Momma, Santa Claus is here!" It was a memory and a look on his face I'll never forget. He was so shocked, and he looked just like a little boy! Marty is gone now, and that will always be one of my favorite memories.

That was our first year that we had Santa visits, and I don't know if it was that year or not, but I think it was—that after Santa was finished and left, that my Uncle Ed showed up for a visit (wink, wink). I will never forget how Sarah, (my niece, Tonya's daughter) ran to him all excited, and told him "Santa was just here! You just missed him, he was here!" Precious.

My Uncle and Aunt told my mom later that that had made it all worth the effort. As the children got older, Santa started looking more and more familiar to them...

Probably my favorite Christmas story of all to share is one that I wasn't even present for. It was a story told to me by my mom. When my mom and dad had only the 3 boys, Kenny, Ricky, and Marty, and Marty was just a baby, things were pretty rough for them that year. My mom told me one time, when I was a very little girl, while we were decorating our tree, why we were using some very different little decorations. The decorations weren't as grand as others, and certainly didn't look store bought. That's because they weren't. These were decorations from many years prior, that she just couldn't bear to let go of, and had kept year after year. Things were rough enough in those days when only my brothers were born, that my mom had cut out very small pieces of thin cardboard into little assorted shapes, wrapped them in tinfoil, then colored the tinfoil, then poked holes in the tops of the shapes and ran a piece of string thru to hang on the tree. They couldn't even afford decorations, so my mom, trying to give brothers the best Christmas that she could, made some homemade decorations. Years later, of course, things got better for them, but momma still kept all those little homemade decorations.

So many more good memories; like the year I wanted a sled so bad, and momma and daddy hid one for me down at my Aunt Peggy's house. I found it by accident, and laid down on it and stayed there the whole duration of our visit. There are also special memories I have of my children's Christmases; of hanging stockings every year for them, and watching them open them all. Silly String was always a must in the stockings, so every year we have silly string fights on Christmas morning. One particular year, when Derek was about 11 years old, he had wanted a trampoline all year long so bad. John and I and the kids had our Christmas and gift opening that morning. When it was over—so the kids thought—John told Derek to go out to his truck and get him something for him. What Derek didn't know was there was a new trampoline in the back of the truck. I'll never forget the look on Derek's face and his reaction when he realized there was a trampoline in the truck. He was so happy. I'm so thankful to have been a part of this Christmas book project. It has caused me to look back over the years and remember so many great memories I'd forgotten over time. God Bless.

By Jeannie Sexton

Kids' First Christmas

Christmas is a wonderful time of the year for many reasons; Christmas carols, Christmas plays, dressing up for Christmas church service, decorating the Christmas tree, eating Christmas dinner, spending time with the family—but the most important reason is taking time to honor the birth of Jesus. I've always been amazed by the miracle birth and everything it means to being a Christian. We obviously know what the Bible tells us about Jesus' birth, and then not much else is mentioned until he turns twelve. I would like know what Jesus first words were—or see him take his first steps, then walk and run.

Our three kids range in age from 22–17 years old. The baby days for Dana and I are behind us, but the memories are still special to us. I sometimes wish we could go back to those times when the kids were little and times seemed simpler.

One of my favorite memories is the first Christmas for each one of my kids. Each of the kids was at different stages of growth for their first Christmas. Kylie was older for her first which meant she was talking, crawling, grabbing, and intrigued by the lights. Drew and Ryan were younger for their first Christmas which meant they were not as intrigued, which would change in years to come. The one thing that was consistent for all three kids was Dana would always buy a Christmas ornament with the year of their birth and hang it on the tree. Until recently I don't think I ever told Dana how much it meant to me to see those ornaments every year hanging on the tree alongside the ornaments I made as a child.

I hope, Lord willing, our kids will follow the same tradition with their children as a reminder of their first Christmas.

By Richard Huerta

Did you know?
All the gifts in the *12 Days of Christmas* would equal 364 gifts.

NOTE:
If you have memories or traditions you would like to share, here are a couple of pages we've left blank for you so you can write on them:

Short Stories (Fiction)

The Best Christmas
By Debbie Stickler

Here I am walking in an alley looking in each trash bin for just a scrap of food. I ask myself *how did I get in this place—what did I do to offend God so bad that all of these bad things are happening to me?*

I was walking behind Spurgeon's Family Café, hoping Mr. Spurgeon had thrown some food away. As I was digging in the trash bin, the back door opened and there stood a plump woman with a kind face. I turned to walk away when she said to me kindly, "Hi, I am Mrs. Spurgeon. Are you hungry?"

I bowed my head, ashamed to look at her; but I nodded my head yes.

She took me into what was the kitchen of that café. Oh, the smell of that place! I saw chicken, ham, sweet potatoes, and corn on the cob; rolls, and hot apple pie. I thought I was in Heaven. As Mrs. Spurgeon talked, my mouth was watering.

She said, "Oh my, where's my manners? Let's get you some food!"

There was a graying older man cooking, she referred to him as *Papa*.

"Papa, we have a visitor," she said, "Can you bring him the biggest steak we have? And don't forget all the fixin's Papa."

Mrs. Spurgeon smiled and nodded as he replied, "Yes, mother."

This couple reminded me of my own parents. As I stood there, my mind drifted back to my childhood. I thought of how we loved each other—and of how that, after chores were done, and supper was finished, my dad would take the old family Bible and read to us.

I shook my head as if trying to clear the cobwebs and thought to myself, *why did dad waste our time with that nonsense of Bible reading? Where was God when my parents died?*

Mr. Spurgeon came and set in front of me the biggest steak I had ever seen. I was just about to take a bite when I heard Mrs. Spurgeon start to pray:

"Lord, we thank you for bringing this young man to our door. I ask You to bless him and keep him safe."

I sat there thinking, *why are you praying to God? He doesn't hear you and He don't care.*

But who was I to tell them that? They were nice—plus they were feeding me.

"Is there any work that I can do to pay for my meal?" I asked. "I have no money."

"There's no need," they assured me.

"Do you have a place to sleep?" Mr. Spurgeon asked.

"Yes, I do," I answered.

"Is it indoors?"

"No."

"You do now," he said.

"Only if I can work for it," I answered.

They smiled at each other.

"In the morning, after breakfast, you can work in the kitchen," said Mrs. Spurgeon.

"Thank you, I would like that," I said.

As I was shown the room where I would be staying, I again told them thank you as I shut the door. I looked around the room and went towards my bed, thinking about how dirty my clothes were—and how clean the bed looked. Oh, a bed! I tried to think how long it had been since I had slept in a bed. About that time, there was a knock on the door; Mr. Spurgeon was there with some clothes in his hands.

"Mother said you may be able to wear these. The bathroom is down the hall; you can clean up there," he said.

I took the clothes, "Thank you!" I said.

I awoke the next morning to the smell of fresh coffee, bacon, and hot rolls. I laid there, almost forgetting about my situation.

I ended up staying with the Spurgeon's for a while and helping in the kitchen every day. The café was open Monday through Saturday. Mr. Spurgeon said we need to keep the Sabbath and give honor to our creator.

Every Sunday, they would go to church, and I would go to the creek.

One Sunday, as I was walking back from the creek, it hit me like a ton of bricks—Christmas was in two weeks! I had been saving my money from working at the café. When I walked in the back door, I could hear Mr. and Mrs. Spurgeon talking softly.

"Mother, I just don't know where we are going to get that extra money. We always help the children at the orphanage at Christmas...I just don't know mother," Mr. Spurgeon said.

"Pa, Jesus always provides for His children—and He will again."

I thought to myself, *I have some money saved. I will give it to the Spurgeon's. I will be meeting their need, not God*—or so I thought.

The time flew by and soon it was Christmas Eve. I took my money to the Spurgeon's and said, "Here, I supplied for this need, not God."

Mrs. Spurgeon looked at me, "No, child, God did supply the need. He just used you to do it."

It dawned on me at that time; that, while I had been angry at God all this time, He had been working things out on my behalf.

I went with the Spurgeon's to the orphanage and saw all the smiles that were brought on by the food and gifts that had been purchased with the money I had saved.

Mrs. Spurgeon looked at me and smiled, "For such a time as this," she said.

Then I knew I needed Jesus in my heart. That was the best Christmas.

The World's Largest Snowman (almost)
By L.D. Lewis

I stepped outside and blinked while shielding my eyes with a gloved hand as the sun reflected blindingly off of the snow. I stomped through the knee-deep snow, pausing occasionally to look back at the huge imprints my boots made with each step.

My feet were already starting to get cold and I wondered if two pairs of socks were enough. A few years ago, when I was about four years old, I almost got frostbite on my toes—it *really* hurt—now that I am ten, I know to go inside if my feet get too cold.

I am going to build the *world's biggest snowman!* People will probably come from all over the world to see it. I am sure the newspaper people will come out and take pictures—and they will want to interview me. I will be friendly to everyone—I will not allow success to go to my head. I will refuse any payment for the pictures. The snowman will be so big that it may never melt—it will probably still be here in the summer time! We can have snowball fights in July if we dare take any snow from the World's Largest Snowman. The President might put armed guards by it to protect it from people who want to take a piece of the snow. You know, when I am famous, I will probably make a lot of money showing other people how to build snowmen...I hope mom and dad are ready for all of the attention.

I looked around for the best place to start. This snowman will probably use all of the snow in my yard—maybe all of the snow in the neighborhood!

"Hey!" my brother shouted at me as he stepped outside.

"What?"

"I thought you were going to build a snowman."

"I am."

"Well quit stomping all over the yard!"

"I'm deciding where to start."

He shook his head. He is seven years older than I am and he thinks he knows everything. He likes girls (yuck!), so he can't be too smart.

"You're messing up the best places to make a snowman," he called as he tugged on his gloves.

Just wait until he sees the huge snowman I am going to build—he won't try to boss me around after that, I'll bet.

"Humph!" I huffed at him.

"Just stay there, I'll help you," he said.

"Help me? Ha!" I grumbled to myself.

"What?" he asked.

"I don't need any help," I answered.

He bent down to lace up his snow boots and I couldn't resist—I scooped up a handful of snow and packed it into a great snowball. I closed one eye and stuck out my tongue while taking careful aim. The snow was too deep for me to do my pitcher's stance, so I had to just lob it at him.

Okay, Murphy's Law says that if something can go wrong, it will—now, with that said, let me explain that as soon as that perfectly shaped snowball left my hand, for some reason, my mom opened the front door—no, the snowball didn't hit her—the snowball sailed right past her and hit our dog!

Our dog was a little Chihuahua. Chihuahua's are a pretty nervous type of dog and you can imagine her surprise at getting plastered by a snowball! I heard her yelp and then I heard something shatter as she skedaddled out of there. And I do mean *out*! She charged out the front door and ran right off of the porch! I laughed out loud when she disappeared under the snow. Every few seconds her nose would pop up again and she would let out a yelp and disappear again, only to pop up again a few feet farther out into the yard.

"Get her!" mom said, pointing at the last place she had disappeared.

I carefully headed for the place I thought she would pop up next, hoping I wouldn't step on her.

"Yelp!" she yelped very near me as her head popped up through the snow. I grabbed for her—and she bit my finger before sinking back down into the snow and disappearing again. Luckily, my gloves protected my fingers. I jammed my hands down under the snow, trying to catch her. She popped up right under my face and snapped at my nose before plopping back under again. I grabbed for her and got hold of her leg. She spun around and clamped her little teeth onto my hand. She was growling when she went out of sight.

"Here, let me get her," my brother said, reaching down into the snow.

"Go ahead, let her bite a chunk out of you," I said.

He found her and gently picked her up. She was calm and relaxed in his hand as he cradled her close to his chest and carried her back toward the house.

She bared her teeth at me as he walked past me.

Mom made me come inside to warm up. Of course I was in trouble for throwing the snowball into the house—

...and the snow melted before I got to build the World's Largest Snowman.

Christmas Filled With Curiosity
By Natalie Conner (Age 13)

"Two days until Christmas!" exclaimed Marianne to her mom, Holly. She was barely able to contain her excitement. "Mom, I thought grandma was supposed to be her by now."

"Honey, I know—they may be stuck in some snow or something. We don't know for sure," said Holly in a worried voice.

"I sure hope not!" exclaimed Marianne as she went back to what she was doing.

After a few hours had passed, and there was still no sign of grandma, Marianne said, "Mom, I'm beginning to worry about grandma."

"Honey, I'm sure she's fine. She said she would be here either today or tomorrow—so maybe she's planning on being here tomorrow instead of today."

"Mom, do you know who else I'm worrying about?"

"Who?" Holly asked curiously.

"Dad," said Marianne.

"I am too, but there's nothing we can do about it except pray that God will keep him safe during his time in the army—and that he will be able to feel our love across the seas. And just remember, Marianne; he will be home in 9 months!"

Holding the locket on her necklace that contained a picture of her dad, Marianne tried to think happy thoughts of that wonderful day to come.

After supper, Holly received a text from her grandma saying that she wouldn't be there until Christmas Day.

Holly was a bit upset because they usually opened gifts on Christmas Eve.

Marianne called her grandma to see why she couldn't be there until Christmas Day, but her grandma didn't give a reason; all she said was, "I'm sorry. I will see you on Christmas Day."

Marianne very sadly made her way to the living room to tell her mom the news.

Her mom seemed a little sad too, but she said, "As long as I get to see her. After baking, wrapping presents, making decorations, putting up the tree—and everything else I have to do for Christmas—I guess I shouldn't complain.

Then came a loud knock on the front door. Marianne ran to the door and looked out the window. It was grandma!

"Grandma! Grandma!" Marianne said when she opened the door. "I am so excited that you are here! You really did surprise me!"

"I'm so glad to be here too," said her grandma.

"Mom would like us to come to the kitchen and start eating with the rest of the family," said Marianne.

Marianne so enjoyed the rest of the eating; the eating and visiting. Then came time for opening presents. Presents upon presents were under the tree, but there was one that was triggering little Marianne's curiosity as to what was inside. She was wondering if it might be for her. As they came to that gift, Marianne was so excited that the name they called was hers! As she opened it, she saw that it contained a smaller box inside. She opened the smaller box from grandma and there was only a note that said:

I couldn't get you much, but I want you to know that I love you so much and I am proud of you and the sweet young lady you have become.

Love, Grandma

"There is a little something for you though in the back of the house. Holly, you should come with us as well. The present is for both of you. We hid it inside the shed because we didn't want you to see us carry it in."

As they made their way to the shed, Marianne and Holly's minds were racing to try to try and figure out what this secret gift was. Marianne and her mother opened up the shed and there was a little box. When they opened it, it had a picture of a large question mark, and it read, "Look to the right."

As Holly and Marianne quickly looked to the right, there was Marianne's dad!

Marianne and her mother burst into tears of joy and gladness that he was home for Christmas—just as Marianne had wished.

Her dad said, "I have both you as a present!" And then he gave them both a huge hug and a kiss.

The family was overjoyed! At the end of the day, they all gathered around the piano to sing Christmas Carols and thank the Lord for her dad's safe trip home from China.

That was the best Christmas ever!

The Christmas Gift
By Dana Huerta

I stood with my nose pressed against the ice cold glass. My heart was overjoyed to see my dad and two older brothers dragging in this year's Christmas tree on an old wagon with the two big draft horses that were my father's pride and joy. My dad was so proud of how those two horses had pulled many a tree out of the hills where we lived in Oklahoma.

Every year I always looked forward to Christmas, our family didn't have much but our gifts were always heartfelt and you knew there was love that went into each one of them. I, being ten years old, and the youngest—not to mention; the *only* girl, had the privilege of helping mother with baking and decorating. My brothers were more fortunate than I since they got to help our dad outside. I loved to be outside but most of all I adored my dad and loved being with him. As I put wood in the fireplace my mind wandered back to the Christmas morning last year as my family gathered round for the reading of the Christmas story. It was a yearly tradition and my father read it straight from the Bible. My parents were wonderful Christian people and Bible reading was a daily routine for our family. Last year's story will forever be engraved in my heart. We all sat and listened very intently as my dad told us about how Jesus came as a babe. Born in a lowly stable amongst the animals and lying in a manger. As I sat and listened, my mind began to imagine being there at the time Jesus was born. I pondered in my heart what gift would I have given the newborn King. About that time my dad caught my attention with the close of the story. It was time for bed for it was Christmas Eve and we would be having friends and family over tomorrow to celebrate the Saviour's birth. As I lay in bed looking at the stars through the window my mind still envisioned how it was at the time of Jesus' birth. That night I dreamed I was actually there in the stable. As I looked at the newborn Saviour, I wondered what gift I could give a King. Everything that I could think of seemed so insignificant. I was so upset when I awoke because I didn't give Jesus anything. Later that morning I was telling my parents what I had dreamed. My dad began to explain that Jesus not only came into this world as a babe but as a Saviour; one who would take away the sins of mankind. My father explained that Jesus was really a gift to us but we had to accept him as our personal Saviour. I was so happy hearing what my dad was saying that it came to me what I could give the Christ Child. Being Christmas Morning it was time to open our gifts I was so excited to see that I had gotten a new doll, an apple, an orange and a shiny new nickel. When we had finished opening our gifts I explained to my parents that there was another gift. I wrapped a box very pretty and put Jesus' Name on the tag. Inside the box was a piece of paper with the word "Myself" written on it, I knew the greatest gift that I could give would be me. I asked Jesus into my heart that Christmas morning.

So you see my heart and life was forever changed by the greatest gift that could ever have been given to mankind. For Jesus is that gift.

Did you know?
Each year more than 3 billion Christmas cards are sent in the United States alone.

Moments of Inspiration

Push On

Push on a little bit longer—
You haven't got long to go
Push on a little bit farther—
You're about at the end of the row
Push on a little bit farther—
And let the sunshine glow.

By Catherine M. Tosh

His Hands

It may not be according to our
wants and plans
But God still has all things in His
hands.

By Catherine M. Tosh

Darla Jo

My story isn't about Christmas; it's about the birth of my first baby girl.

We were thrilled when it came time for Darla Jo to be born. She came a little early; she was due in February, but was born December 30th. After she was born, they took me to my room. With this being my first child, I didn't know that they would let you see the baby before they took it to the nursery. I didn't see her that day—or the next day either. I knew I had a lot of visitors; but, being young, I thought the visitors were there to see me and my baby.

I went into the waiting room where my family was sitting. They were all waiting to see our baby.

I told them that I had gotten cheated again—that they didn't bring her to me.

About that time, a doctor came in. "*You* got cheated," he said sarcastically.

Without trying to spare our feelings at all, he told us that our baby was born with a birth defect called Spina

Bifida. She had a hole in her back that would have to be closed. He advised against surgery—in other words, just let her die.

I'm so thankful that my dad was there. My husband and I didn't quite understand—my dad did; he said, "You want them to sign her death certificate? No! They will give her every chance they can to make sure she lives!"

After surgery, the surgeon said, "If she lives—kids born with this condition don't usually live past five years of age."

That was in December. We didn't get to bring her home until April. I'm so thankful that God saw fit to allow us to have her for sixteen years—she was a treasure!

My mom was a Christian. She was a real grandma to Darla Jo. My dad wasn't saved, but he sure helped with her.

Darla Jo never walked, but was as smart as she could be. You could give her a phone number and tell her to remember it; two or three weeks later, she could tell it to you. She never wrote it down, it was in her memory.

I know she's in Heaven with Jesus; walking with her dad, granny, and granddad.

There's so much more I could tell. She always had a smile on her face. When people met her, they always left happy. Even though she couldn't walk, that didn't stop her from being a very sweet and happy girl. God blessed us when he gave her to us.

He also gave her two precious sisters who she loved very much. They know one day we will all be together if we keep Jesus in our hearts. I believe Darla Jo will run to meet us. I believe she is saying, "Come on! You can make it—I did!"

By Sis. Sue Young

The Messiah

Some people ask how we know that Jesus is the Messiah. We know, in part, because of the specific prophecies given in the Bible that were fulfilled by Jesus—or because of Him. There is a two-part reason for the prophecies: one is to prove the accuracy of the scriptures; the other is to specify, to the fine detail, the lineage and life of the Messiah. Any deviation from the prophecies would prove either the prophecy or the Messiah to be false. Take a look at the following prophecies and I think you'll agree that the prophecies were true—and that Jesus is the Messiah:

    Would be the Seed of a Woman
        Prophecy: Genesis 3:15
        Fulfilled: Galatians 4:4

    Promised Seed of Abraham
        Prophecy: Genesis 18:18
        Fulfilled: Acts 3:25

    Promised to be of Isaac's lineage
        Prophecy: Genesis 17:19
        Fulfilled: Matthew 1:2

    Promised Seed of Jacob
        Prophecy: Numbers 24:17
        Fulfilled: Luke 3:24

    From the Tribe of Judah
        Prophecy: Genesis 49:10
        Fulfilled   Luke 3:33

    Heir to the Throne of David
        Prophecy: Isaiah 9:7
        Fulfilled: Matthew 1:1

Birthplace
    Prophecy: Micah 5:2
    Fulfilled: Matthew 2:1

Time of Birth
    Prophecy: Daniel 9:25
    Fulfilled: Luke 2:1-2

Born of a Virgin
    Prophecy: Isaiah 7:14
    Fulfilled: Matthew 1:18

Infants killed (effort to kill the newborn king)
    Prophecy: Jeremiah 31:15
    Fulfilled: Matthew 2:16

Flight into Egypt
    Prophecy: Hosea 11:1
    Fulfilled: Matthew 2:14

Ministry in Galilee
    Prophecy: Isaiah 9:1-2
    Fulfilled: Matthew 4:12-16

Would be a Prophet
    Prophecy: Deuteronomy 18:15
    Fulfilled: John 6:14

A Priest, after the order of Melchizedek
    Prophecy: Psalm 110:4
    Fulfilled: Hebrews 6:20

Rejected by the Jews
    Prophecy: Isaiah 53:3
    Fulfilled: John 1:11

He Would Be Wise
  Prophecy: Isaiah 11:2
  Fulfilled: Luke 2:52

Triumphant Entry into Jerusalem
  Prophecy: Zechariah 9:9
  Fulfilled: John 12: 13-14

Betrayed by a Friend
  Prophecy: Psalm 41:9
  Fulfilled: Mark 14:10

Sold for 30 Pieces of Silver
  Prophecy: Zechariah 11:12
  Fulfilled: Matthew 26:15

The Betrayal Money returned for a Potter's Field
  Prophecy: Zechariah 11:13
  Fulfilled: Matthew 27:6-7

Judas replaced
  Prophecy: Psalm 100:7-8
  Fulfilled: Acts 11:18-20

Falsely Accused
  Prophecy: Psalm 27:12
  Fulfilled: Matthew 26:60-61

Silent before His Accusers
  Prophecy: Isaiah 53:7
  Fulfilled: Matthew 26:62-63

Smitten and Spat Upon
  Prophecy: Isaiah 50:6
  Fulfilled: Mark 14:65

Hated without a Cause
    Prophecy: Psalm 69:4
    Fulfilled: John 15:23-25

Suffered in Our Place
    Prophecy: Isaiah 53:4-5
    Fulfilled: Matthew 8:16-17

Crucified with Sinners
    Prophecy: Isaiah 53:12
    Fulfilled: Matthew 27:38

Hands and Feet Pierced
    Prophecy: Psalm 22:16
    Fulfilled: John 20:27

Mocked and Despised
    Prophecy: Psalm 22:6-8
    Fulfilled: Matthew 27:39-40

Given Gall and Vinegar
    Prophecy: Psalm 69:21
    Fulfilled: John 19:20

Prophetic Words used to mock Him
    Prophecy: Psalm 22:8
    Fulfilled: Matthew 27:43

Prays for His Enemies
    Prophecy: Psalm 109:4
    Fulfilled: Luke 23:34

His Side Pierced
    Prophecy: Zechariah 12:10
    Fulfilled: John 19:34

Lots Cast for His Coat
   Prophecy: Psalm 22:18
   Fulfilled: Mark 15:24

Not a Bone to be Broken
   Prophecy: Psalm 34:20
   Fulfilled: John 19:33

Buried with the Rich
   Prophecy: Isaiah 53:9
   Fulfilled: Matthew 27:57-60

Resurrected from the Dead
   Prophecy: Psalm 16:10
   Fulfilled: Matthew 28:9

Would Ascend back into Heaven
   Prophecy: Psalm 68:18
   Fulfilled: Luke 24:50-51

Rapture (Return of Christ)
   Prophecy: 1Thessalonians 4:16-17
   NOT YET FULFILLED!

This partial list of fulfilled prophecies regarding Jesus should remind us that there is another prophecy that has not yet happened—the prophecy concerning His imminent return for those who are saved. It is real. And it could happen at any time. Are you ready?

By L.D. Lewis

Choices

There are two things in life that we don't get to choose: our birth and our death.

Jesus had a choice. He *chose* to take on the form of man and be born in a lowly stable. He chose to suffer pain, heartache, sickness and sorrow—in the end, He *chose* to die in our place. No one made Him. It was a choice. Because of His choice, we now have the hope of eternal life—but we must make the most important choice of our life; will we choose life or death?

Just as sure as we were born, we will die. What we do in between is our choice. We must make the right choice. It is a life or death decision. I choose life! I choose Jesus! Won't you?

"And as it is appointed unto man once to die, but after this the judgment." Hebrews 9:27

"Jesus saith unto him, I am the way, the truth, and the life: no man cometh unto the Father but by me." John 14:16

"For God so loved the world, that he gave his only begotten Son, that whosoever believeth in him should not perish, but have everlasting life." John 3:16

By Charity Lewis

Who is Jesus?

Zoologists call Him
the **Lion of Judah**.
Botanists call Him the
Tree of Life.
Geologists call Him the
Rock of Ages.
Cooks call Him the
Bread of Life.
Mathematicians call Him the
Alpha and Omega
Engineers call Him a
Strong Tower
Doctors call Him the
Great Healer.
I call Him **Saviour**.

Did you know?
Silent Night was first sung as part of a church service in Austria. A guitar was used to accompany the singer because the church organ was so badly rusted it couldn't be played.

What a Precious Gift!

God gave a gift—
He gave it to men
It was despised
and rejected by them:

Eternal life
sent from above
God gave His best
and wrapped it in love
What a precious gift!

Men took the gift
They tore off the bow
They ripped the paper
They did not know:

It was
Eternal life
sent from above
God gave His best
and wrapped it in love
What a precious gift!

Now the package is torn
You can see what's inside
God's love for man
The gift is yours tonight:

Eternal life
sent from above
God gave His best
and wrapped it in love
What a precious gift!

Now that you know
God's gift for you
You have a choice
What will you do?

With
Eternal life
sent from above
God gave His best
and wrapped it in love
What a precious gift!

By L.D. Lewis

The Gift of Joy

While working in a retail store; closer and closer to Christmas season I have noticed how different people's attitudes can be. Some seem happy and easy to please, some seem unhappy and impossible to please—and others just nonchalantly roam the store somehow expressing very little personality whatsoever—but that's beside the point.

People have a rather large effect on other people and the attitudes of those they interact with, whether they realize it or not. Have you noticed when somebody smiles and greets you it is a natural reaction to smile and greet them in return?

A cheerful attitude is contagious and is easily spread from one person to another, but so is a grouchy one. Walking around with a sour look on my face and a grouchy attitude when interacting with strangers can put a damper on someone's mood or even their day without me even realizing it. But with a joyful expression, a quick smile and a friendly and cheerful attitude, someone's mood or day could be changed and it might even leave a lasting impression on them. You only get one chance at a first impression, and, as a Christian, I want people's first impression to be the joy I have in my life because of Jesus. So many people are hurting, even during the Christmas season, and they may seem unappeasable and irritable but there is no telling what difficulties they may be facing in their lives. A smile and a friendly attitude might be the Christmas gift somebody needs to lighten their mood and add a little joy to their day.

By Kyle Lewis

Lost Opportunity

Mommy, watch me!
the little girl cried
See what I can do?
It's almost Christmas, mommy
Look what I made for you!
What are you looking at, mommy?
Can I see?
Why are you looking at your phone, mommy
instead of looking at me?

Daddy look!
said the little boy
Can we buy a kite?
...Daddy? ...Daddy?
Oh well, it's alright.
What are you looking at daddy?
Can I see?
Why are you looking at your phone, daddy
Instead of talking to me?

By L.D. Lewis

Did you know?
The first printed reference to a Christmas tree was in 1531 in Germany.

Christmas Memories

Christmas memories?
Oh yes! Many I can remember!
Anticipation! Keeping secrets
through all those Decembers.
That time of the year
filled with wonder and joy.
Such a magical time
for little girls and little boys!
The memory of momma
in the kitchen at night,
Smell the hot chocolate, and cookies
to eat by Christmas tree lights?
How much longer to wait?
Will it ever get here?
That big red box
has MY name on it right there!
Yes, precious memories
of loved ones and gifts
and so much food as the heart pleases
but let's never forget the reason,
and that reason is Jesus!

By Jeannie Sexton

Did you know?
Christmas purchases account for 1/6 of all retail sales in the United States each year.

Do you have a Christmas Poem or Inspired Thought of your own? Here's a place for you to write it down:

Recipes

Mama always made "Sandies" at Christmas. It became my favorite cookie. I don't remember a Christmas that I haven't made these simple yet delicious little cookies and I always think of mama when I make them.

Christmas Sandies

- 1 c. butter
- 1/3 c. sugar
- 2 tsp. water
- 2 tsp. vanilla
- 2 c. flour
- 1 c. chopped pecans

Mix well. Form into small balls and flatten out to make small round cookies (about 1-1/2" round).

Bake at 350° for 20 minutes. Roll in powdered sugar.
Let cool before stacking. Store in an airtight container.

By Charity Lewis

My late husband, Johnny, had a favorite dish that we still make every Thanksgiving and Christmas. It was handed down from his Grandma Young, and Johnny's mother taught me how to make it. Here it is:

Granny Young's Fruit Salad

5 or 6 apples (leave peeling on)
5 or 6 oranges, peeled
5 or 6 bananas, peeled
Chop oranges, apples, and bananas in large bowl.
Mix together 1½ cups sugar, 2/3 cups Milnot, 1½ cups Mayo.
Mix well, and then pour over fruit. Stir well.
You can add walnuts or pecans if desired.

This has long been a family tradition of the Young Family.

By Sis. Sue Young

Cocoa Surprise

We live in a very small house, but that doesn't stop our family from getting together on Christmas Day. There are 28 people in our immediate family that come to our house every year. That doesn't count the guests that they bring with them. You could say we are a "close" family.

Every year for dinner we usually have pretty much the same food: turkey, ham, gravy, cornbread dressing, cranberry sauce, sweet potato casserole—and whatever new dish we want to try. Oh! Don't forget the rolls!

We always have pumpkin pie, and what we call **Cocoa Surprise** (and, again, whatever new desserts we want to try).

We always have so much food that everyone gets to take leftovers home.

Cocoa Surprise

1st layer:

Knead together by hand:
1 cup flour
1 stick butter
1 cup chopped pecans

Spread in a 9x13 greased pan. (Do not flour). Bake at 350° for 20 minutes. Let cool.

2nd layer:

1 large package softened cream cheese
½ large carton Cool Whip
1 cup powdered sugar

Knead with hands and spread carefully onto crust.

3rd layer:

1 large package instant vanilla pudding
1 large package instant chocolate pudding
4½ cups milk
With mixer, blend together.

4th layer:

Add the other ½ of Cool Whip plus small container of Cool Whip. Sprinkle chopped pecans on top. Refrigerate.

By Douglas and Linda Farmer

My Favorite Recipes for Christmas Time
(By Sister Stephanie Conner)

Wassail

Mix in Crockpot (or stove top): 1 Gal. Apple Cider, 8 cinnamon sticks, 1 quart pineapple juice, 1 can frozen orange juice, allspice and ground cinnamon to taste. Top with sliced oranges studded with 27 whole cloves to float on top. Cook until hot, serve and enjoy!

> Did you know?
> Wassail is from the Old Norse *Ves Heil*, meaning "good health".

Kimmie's Cheese Log

Mix and roll in wax paper to shape and store: 1 lb. Velveeta, 1 cup pecans, 4 oz. cream cheese, ½ tsp. garlic powder, ½ tsp. red pepper. Makes 1 log

Nannie's Punch

Pour into punch bowl, I Gallon <u>Fruit Punch Kool-Aid</u> (frozen till slushy), add equal parts of cold (or slushy) Cola and <u>Ginger Ale</u> to fill punch bowl.

Easy Snow Ice Cream

8 Cups <u>snow</u> or shaved ice, 1 14 oz. can of <u>sweetened condensed milk</u> and 1 tsp. <u>vanilla extract</u>. Mix and enjoy!!

Spicy Ranch Crackers

Mix 1 ½ Cups <u>Canola oil</u>, 2 <u>Tbsp. Crushed red pepper</u> and 1 package <u>Hidden Valley dry ranch mix</u> in a 1 gallon Ziploc bag. Add 1 box <u>saltines crackers</u> and mix well. Make sure all crackers get covered with mixture. Spread out on wax paper to dry for 2-3 hours.

Lil Smokies

Put 2 packages of lil smokies, ½ cup mustard and 1 jar of grape jelly into a crockpot and cook on low for about 4 hours or on high for 1 ½ hours.

Teriyaki Meatballs

I make this recipe in a crockpot but it can also be baked as well. Mix 2 bags original meatballs, 2 lb. bag of brown sugar, 2 bottles of teriyaki sauce (the one with seeds on top), 2 cans pineapple chunks and ½ each of red, yellow and green bell peppers, diced. Cook in crockpot until heated through or in oven at 400 degrees until heated through.

Cheesy Gift Dip

Mix ½ tsp. dried dill, ¼ tsp. garlic powder, and 1/8 tsp. salt into an 8oz. block of softened cream cheese. Put plastic wrap into cream cheese box and put mixture back in to mold. Decorate top with red bell pepper to look like a gift or shred a little bit of the red bell pepper and put into mixture before shaping. Eat with crackers of choice.

Pecan Pie Mixture

Makes 3 pecan pies or 32 mini pies

Melt 2 sticks margarine and set aside. Prepare 16 oz. pecans. Chop finely for the mini pies (premade tart shells). Put 16 oz. brown sugar into large mixing bowl and work out any lumps with the back of a spoon. Add 1 heaping Tbsp. self-rising flour and stir until flour disappears. Add 16 oz. bottle of corn syrup (light or dark, which ever you prefer), and 1 Tbsp. Vanilla extract. Stir until combined. Add melted butter and stir until it's all worked in. In a separate bowl, crack 6 eggs, remove the roosters and whip. Fold eggs into pie mixture until they disappear. Put pecans in the bottom of each pie and pour mixture over them. The pecans will float up as they cook. Bake regular pies at 350 degrees for 50-60 minutes. Bake mini pies at 350 for approximately 40 minutes. Remove and let cool to set. I like to wrap the mini pies in saran wrap and put a miniature bow on top to give as a treat to each of our church members at Christmas time.

Red Hot Pepper Jam

Wash, seed and cut 3 small red bell peppers and 3 jalapeño peppers into smaller pieces. Put into blender to finely chop. It should measure about 1 ½ cups. In 8 quart saucepan combine peppers, 3 cups sugar, 1 cup light corn syrup, ¾ cup cider vinegar, and ½ tsp. salt. Stirring frequently, bring to a full rolling boil over high heat. Stirring constantly, boil for 5 minutes. Remove from heat. Stir in 1 pouch (3oz) liquid pectin until well blended. With metal spoon, skim off the foam.

Ladle into clean, hot ½ pint jars, leaving ½ inch head space. Wipe top edge with damp cloth. Place sterilized <u>lids</u> and <u>rings</u> on and process in a water bath for 10 minutes. Cool on wire rack or folded towel. To prevent floating peppers, turn jars upside down after about 15 minutes cooling and then turn back right side up and allow to finish cooling. The cans should start popping to seal. Serve with crackers. Makes about 5 jars

For green pepper jam: Follow recipe except omit the red bell peppers. Use 3 large green bell peppers. If desired, add 2-3 drops of green food color with pectin.

For yellow pepper jam: Use yellow bell peppers and yellow food coloring.

Apple Cider Donuts

Mix in a large bowl: 3 ¼ cups <u>all-purpose flour</u>, 2/3 cup <u>sugar</u>, 2 tsp. <u>baking powder</u>, 1 ½ tsp. <u>cinnamon</u>, 1 tsp. <u>ground nutmeg</u> and 1 tsp. <u>salt</u>. Mix in 2 <u>eggs</u>, 2/3 cup <u>apple cider</u>, 4 Tbsp. melted <u>butter</u> and 1 tsp. <u>vanilla</u>. Turn out the dough onto a floured surface. Pat to ½ inch thickness. Cut with a donut cutter. Heat 2 inches of cooking oil to 350 degrees. Carefully place donuts into hot oil. Cook 3-4 minutes then turn and cook an additional 3-4 minutes. Yum!!

Candy Cane Crunch

Crush candy canes in a food processor, or in a Ziploc bag with a rolling pin, until it measures about 2 cups. Melt 24 oz. vanilla or almond bark in microwave on high for 2 minutes, stirring often. Stir in crushed candy canes and pour the mixture into a jelly roll pan. Let the candy cool. Break into pieces and place in a cellophane bag, tie with a pretty ribbon and bless someone this Christmas!!

Candy Cane Cappuccino Mixture

Blend 1 cup powdered non-dairy creamer, 1 1/3 cups sugar, 1 cup instant coffee, 1 cup hot cocoa mix in a blender or food processor until a smooth powder results. Store in bag, or container. Mix 1 Tbsp. of mixture into 1 cup boiling water whenever you're ready for a good ole cup of cappuccino and hang a candy cane over the side to stir it with.

Frosty Punch

Combine 3 pkg. <u>unsweetened Kool-Aid</u> (any flavor), 3 cups <u>sugar</u> and 1 46 oz. can of <u>pineapple juice</u> in a large bowl that can be sealed and frozen. Add 2 ½ quarts <u>water</u> and freeze until slushy. Refrigerate until serving time. Add 2 bottles <u>lemon lime soda</u> (sprite) just before serving. Use any color Kool-Aid to match whatever theme you have.

Did you know?
Leftovers can sometimes be your enemy. Spoilt leftovers are responsible for about 400,000 cases of post-Christmas associated illnesses.

Gingerbread
(100 year old recipe)

This recipe has been handed down from my great, great, great Grandmother, Mary Clementine Campbell Howell

Cream 1 ½ cups sugar, 1 cup of butter, 5 eggs (beaten), and 2 cups sorghum. Mix well. Add the following dry ingredients and 1 tsp. soda dissolved in ½ cup sweet milk alternately. 3 cups flour, 1 tsp. ginger, 1 tsp. soda, 1 tsp. ground cloves, 1 tsp. cinnamon, and ¼ tsp. salt. Mix well. Pour into flat greased pan. Bake at 350 degrees for 30 minutes. Cool and cut.

Hello Dollies

One of my Mom's Christmas specialties

Melt 1 cup butter in a 9x13 pan. Sprinkle 1 ½ cups graham cracker crumbs in pan over butter. Add 1 large eagle brand milk, 6 oz. chocolate chips and top with 1 large can of coconut and 1 cup chopped pecans. Bake at 350 degrees for 25-30 minutes. Cool and cut into squares.

Cornbread Salad

Mix 1 box Jiffy Mix and ½ can of Rotel. Bake in a 9x9 pan and bake according to Jiffy bread instructions. Let cool and crumble into bottom of trifle bowl. Mix 1 can of drained corn and 1 large can of pinto beans and spread onto cornbread. Put down a layer of shredded cheddar cheese. For next layer, make a mixture of 16 oz. sour cream, ½ cup miracle whip and 1 pkg. dry ranch mix. Last of all, cut up 3 green onions, ½ bell pepper, 3 roma tomatoes and a bag of real bacon bits. Mix and spread over salad and top with a little more shredded cheese for looks.

Busy Day Chicken

Scatter 1 box of Rice-a-Roni on bottom of greased 9x13 pan. Arrange boneless skinless chicken breast or thighs on top of rice. Combine 1 can cream of mushroom soup and 1 ½ cups of water and seasoning from rice box. Pour over chicken and cook for 2 hours at 325 degrees *Crockpot Chicken and Stuffing*

Layer 4 boneless skinless chicken breasts, 2 boxes chicken flavored stuffing, mix 1 large can of cream of mushroom and 1 cup sour cream and layer. Top with 1 small bag of frozen green beans and add 1 cup water on top. Cook on low for 4 hours, or until chicken is done and water is absorbed.

Peanut Butter Fudge

Bring 2 cups sugar and ½ cup milk to a boil. Boil for about 2 ½ minutes. Remove from heat and stir in 1 tsp. vanilla and ¾ cup peanut butter. Pour into pan lined with wax paper hanging over edge to help remove. Cut into squares when set.

Diet Cobbler

Layer 2 pkgs. Frozen berries of choice, 2 cake mixes and 2 cans of sprite. Bake at 350 degrees for 5o minutes.

Christmas Shake

Combine equal amounts of eggnog and peppermint ice cream in a frosty glass. Stir and enjoy!!

Rosie's Fruit Salad

Mix 1 cup sour cream and 16 oz. cool whip. Add 1 pkg. of Jell-O (any flavor) and stir well. Add 1 large can of fruit cocktail (drained), marshmallows and 1 cup chopped pecans. Chill and serve.

Green Bean Casserole

Mix 1 can cream of mushroom, ½ cup milk, 1 tsp. soy sauce, dash of pepper, 4 cups green beans and 2/3 cup French fried onions and put in 9x13 pan. Bake for 25 minutes at 350 degrees. Stir, Sprinkle rest of French fried onions on top and bake for 5 more minutes.

Oreo Balls

Crush 1 pkg. Oreo cookies. Mix with 1 pkg. softened cream cheese. Form into balls and put into icebox until firm. Dip in melted chocolate and put on wax paper to harden.

Pumpkin Pie

Preheat oven to 425 degrees. Mix together: 1 16oz. can of pumpkin, 1 14 oz. sweetened condensed milk, 2 eggs, 1 tsp. cinnamon. ½ tsp. each of ginger, nutmeg and salt. Pour into 9" pie shell and bake for 15 minutes. Reduce heat to 350 degrees and bake for another 45 minutes.

Cheesy Broccoli Potato Soup

Melt 4 Tbsp. butter in a large sauce pan over medium heat. Add 1 cup chopped onion and cook until tender. Add ½ cup flour, stir until blended. Gradually stir in 4 cups low sodium chicken broth. Heat until slightly thickened. Add 4 cups fat free milk. 16 oz. frozen chopped broccoli and 2 cups peeled, diced potatoes. Cover and cook on low heat for about 15 minutes or until veggies are tender. Stir in 1 ½ cups shredded cheddar cheese, 1 Tbsp. Worcestershire sauce and salt and pepper to taste.

> Did you know?
> In 1962, the first Christmas postage stamp was issued.

Corn Dip

Mix 3 cans Mexicorn, 1 4oz. can green diced chilies (drained), 5 chopped green onions, 1 chopped jalapeño pepper, ¾ cup mayonnaise and 10 oz. shredded cheddar cheese. Serve with Fritos.

Taco Dip

Mix 8 oz. <u>sour cream</u>, 8 oz. <u>whipped cream cheese</u>, 1 pkg. <u>taco seasoning</u>, 4 oz. can chopped <u>jalapeños</u> and ¾ tsp. <u>garlic powder with parsley</u>. Good with tortilla chips.

Chili Cheese Dip

Boil together: 1 15 oz. can of Chili with beans, ½ can of Rotel and 1 cup water. Stir in 2 cups uncooked minute rice and ½ lb. Velveeta cheese. Serve with chips of choice

Billie's Cornbread Dressing

(My mom's dressing is always the highlight of our Christmas Dinner)

Ahead of time: Make 2 9x13 pans of white cornmeal cornbread. Boil and debone1 large bag of chicken pieces. Set meat aside.

Add to broth: salt and pepper to taste, 1 tsp. garlic powder, 1 tsp. rosemary, 3 tsp. sage, 2 tsp. celery seed, 1 tsp. oregano, 1 tsp. parsley, ¼ cup chicken base, 1/3 cup butter, ½ head of chopped celery and 1 diced onion. After onions and celery are tender, add 1 Large can of Cream of Mushroom. Stir and put chicken back in broth.

In a separate bowl: put 5 slices of bread, 5 eggs and 1 cup of milk and let soften.

In large Pan: Crumble cornbread, pour milk and egg mixture over and mix.

Last of all: Pour broth and chicken over mixture until right consistency and texture. Mix well, fold in 4-5 boiled eggs and bake at 375 degrees for about an hour.

Stephanie's Brown Gravy Roast

Place an 11-12 lb. butt or picnic roast in the middle of a roaster oven.

Cut and dice up a 5 lb. bag yellow or red potatoes. No need to peel. Mix with 2 lb. bag of baby carrots and 2 sliced onions and place around roast. Mix 2 packages of Lipton onion soup mix, and about 10 packages of brown gravy mix with enough water to almost completely cover the roast. Cook on 250 degrees overnight. Remove bones. Meat should just fall apart. Stir meat and veggies around to mix. If you want it a little thicker, just add a little cornstarch and water and let boil for a few minutes. I usually start it around 11 p.m. and it is ready by 11 the next morning and ready to just keep warm till lunch time. You can always kick up the temperature to 350 degrees and cook within 6 hours or so.

No Peek Stew

Preheat oven to 275 degrees. Spray a 9x13 dish with cooking spray. Add 2 lbs. stew meat, 2-3 peeled and diced potatoes, 1 bag of sliced carrots and 1 large diced onion. Season with salt and pepper and toss together. Dump 1 15 oz. can of green beans, liquid and all, over the meat and vegetables. Lastly, pour 1 15 oz. can of tomato soup and 1 15 oz. can of cream of mushroom over top. Gently combine with a spoon. Tightly cover with foil. Place casserole dish on a cookie sheet in case it overflows. Bake at 275 degrees for about 4 ½ hours, or until everything is tender. Don't peek!!

Zach's Microwave Fudge

3 cups semi-sweet chocolate chips
1 14oz. can sweetened condensed milk
¼ cup butter
1 tsp. vanilla
¼ tsp. salt

Prepare an 8x8 pan by lining it with foil. Spray with nonstick cooking oil. In a large microwaveable bowl, combine first three ingredients and microwave to melt (about 2-3 minutes). Stir then add vanilla and salt. Stir until smooth. Pour in pan. Put in refrigerator for at least 2 hours. Cut and serve! Store in refrigerator.

By Zach Conner (Age 11)

Write your own recipes:

A note from our Pastor

How About This Season?

There are many different greetings, slogans, that people all around the world use to make on a Christmas card. I love the Christmas season. There are many people in the world that do not believe in Jesus Christ, Emmanuel, God is with us, but they sure like to buy all the gifts that come in this Christmas season. I particularly love this certain slogan, "Jesus is the reason for the season." This is Jesus' season.

We always tell of the story of the birth of Jesus. In the fullness of time an Angel came down from the great Throne of Light to a virgin kneeling in prayer, to ask her if she was willing to give to God a human nature. Her answer was that she "knew not a man" and therefore could not be the mother of the "Expected of nations"

There can never be a birth without love. In this the maiden was right. The conception of new life require the fires of love. But besides the human passion which begets life, there is the passionless passion and wild tranquility of the Holy Ghost, and this is overshadowed the woman and begot in her Emmanuel. At that moment that Mary pronounced Fiat or be it done, something greater happened than the Fiat lux (Let there be light) of creation. For the light that was now made was not the sun, but the Son of God in the flesh. Halleluiah! By pronouncing Fiat, Mary achieved the full role of womanhood, namely to bear the bearer of God's gifts to man. Children come into the world not always as a result of a distinct act of love of man and woman. Though the love between the two be willed, the fruit of their love, which is the child, is not willed in the same way as their love for another. There is an undetermined in human love. The parents do not know whether the child will be a boy or a girl, or the exact time of its birth. Children are later accepted and loved by their parents, but they never directly willed into being by them. But in the Annunciation, the Child was not accepted in any unforeseen way, the Child was willed! Other mothers become conscious of motherhood through physical changes within them, but Mary became conscious through a spiritual change brought on by the Holy Ghost.

As the fall of man was a free act, so too the redemption had to be free. What is called the Annunciation was actually God asking the free consent of a creature to help Him to be incorporated into humanity.

Is there any way to restore harmony to the world? It can be done only by someone coming in from eternity and stopping the note in its wild flight. But will it be a false note? The harmony can be destroyed on one condition only. Of that note is made the first note in a new melody, and then it will become harmonious.

This is precisely what happened when Christ was born. There had been a false note of moral discord introduced by the first man which infected all humanity. God could have ignored it, but it would have been a violation of justice for Him to do so; which is, of course, unthinkable. What he did was to ask a woman, representing humanity, freely to give Him a human nature with which He would start a new humanity. As there was an old humanity in Adam, so there would be a new humanity in Christ. When the angel appeared to Mary, God was announcing this love for the new humanity. It was the beginning of a new earth.

For the nine months that He was cloistered within her, all the food, the wheat, the grapes that she consumed served as a kind of natural Eucharist, passing into Him who later on was to declare that He was the Bread and the Wine of Life. After her nine months were over, the fitting place for Him to be born was in Bethlehem, which means, "House of Bread." When the Divine Child was conceived, Mary's humanity gave Him hands and feet, eyes, and ears, and a body with which to suffer. When she finally gave birth, it was as if a great ciborium had opened, she was holding in her fingers the Guest who was also the Host of the World, as if to say, "Look, this is the Lamb of God, look this is He who takes away the sins of the world.

In the filthiest place of the world, a stable, Purity was born. He, who later to be slaughtered by men acting as beast, was born among beast. He, who calls himself the living bread descended from heaven, was laid in a manger, literally, a place to eat.

There was no room in the inn, but there was room in the stable. The inn is the gathering place of public opinion, the focal point of the world's moods, the rallying place of the popular and the successful. But the stable is a place for the outcast, the ignored, and the forgotten. The world might have expected the Son of God to be born, if He was to be born at all, in an inn. A stable would be the last place in the world where one would have looked for Him. Divinity is always where one least expects to find it.

He was already bearing His cross, the only cross a Babe could bear; a cross of poverty, exile and limitation. His sacrificial intent already shown forth in the message the angels sang to the hills of Bethlehem.

Luke 2:11 *"For unto is born this day in the city of David, a Saviour, which is Christ the Lord."* The word became flesh. Oh praise the Lord! He is the reason for the season. Jesus is the reason.

What are you going to do with this Jesus, in this season? Let him become the Saviour of your heart.

Romans 3:10 *As it is written, there is none righteous, no, not one.*

Romans 3:23 *For all have sinned and come short of the glory God.*

Romans 5:12 *Wherefore as by one man's sin entered into the world, and death by sin, and so death passed upon all men, for that all have sinned.*

Romans 6:23 *For the wages of sin is death, but the gift of God is eternal life through Jesus Christ our Lord.*

Romans 5:8 *But God commendeth his love toward us, in that while we were yet sinners Christ died for us.*

Romans 10:9-10 *That if thou shalt confess with thy mouth, the Lord Jesus, and shalt believe in thine heart that God hath raised him from the dead, thou shalt be saved. For with the heart the mouth confession is made unto salvation.*

Romans 10:13 *For whosoever shall call on the name of the Lord shall be saved.*

Let Christ be the Reason for the Season this season.

Merry Christmas!

Pastor Nathan Conner

Made in the USA
San Bernardino, CA
08 November 2015